Y0-BOC-643

REINCARNATION

(Theosophical Manual No. 2)

Reincarnation

A Lost Chord in Modern Thought

By
LEOLINE L. WRIGHT

Published for POINT LOMA PUBLICATIONS, INC.
by
THE THEOSOPHICAL PUBLISHING HOUSE
Wheaton, Ill., U.S.A.
Madras India / London, England

Wright, Leoline L
. Reincarnation.

    1. Reincarnation. I. Title.
BP573.R5W72   129'.4   74-18350
ISBN 0-8356-0453-5

The Theosophical Publishing House,
Wheaton, Illinois 60187,
a department of The Theosophical Society in America

Printed in the United States of America

CONTENTS

EDITORS' PREFACE

Nature exists and Man exists, and somewhere, undisguised by man's own sophistry, there must be available the wisdom and learning which tells us *why* and *how*. As we ponder the question it seems an inevitable conclusion that somewhere there must be preserved a recording, a gathering of facts or "laws," a formulation in human language, of the truth concerning Man and Nature. There must be a basic source from which sciences, philosophies and great religions have sprung.

H. P. Blavatsky, in her writings of immense intellectual and spiritual force and power—still not fully appreciated—points to that Source. She called it the Ancient Wisdom, the Sacred Science, the *Gupta-Vidya,* and gave to it the Greek name of *Theosophia,* Theosophy, knowledge and wisdom such as the gods or divinities live by. This Ancient Wisdom, she declared, has always been in existence, though not always publicly known, having come down the ages tested and checked by generations of Great Seers. It may be called the Facts of Being, the "laws" or workings of Nature.

In this series of twelve Theosophical Manuals, this Ancient Wisdom is explained with clarity of presentation and logical appeal by students and scholars who have devoted a lifetime to theosophic study. Above all they have been governed by strict honesty and adherence to the teachings as originally reported and recorded.

The first booklet, *What Is Theosophy?: A General View For Inquirers,* outlines the over-all teachings, presenting a general picture. Succeeding booklets cover in greater detail the subjects of Reincarnation, Karma, The Seven Principles of Man, Death and the After-Death States of Consciousness, Evolution, Man's Divine Parentage: the Origin of Man and of the Earth, The Doctrine of Cycles, The Ladder of Life: Hierarchies, The Astral Light, Psychic Powers, and Theosophy and Christianity.

It is hoped that these Studies will be received with an open mind, for in them the earnest searcher will find keys that are indispensable to an understanding of the Universe and of Man.

Helen Todd
W. Emmett Small

I know that I am deathless,
I know this orbit of mine cannot be swept by a
     carpenter's compass. . . .
Births have brought us richness and variety
And other births will bring us richness
     and variety.
And as to you, Life, I reckon you are the
     leavings of many deaths.
(No doubt I have died myself ten thousand
     times before.)

—Walt Whitman
"Song of Myself "

I
REIMBODIMENT A HABIT OF NATURE

A characteristic viewpoint of Theosophy is that man is a deathless, spiritual Ego using mind and body as a garment, or as its vehicle of expression and experience in the external world. The present general tendency to regard ourselves as the product simply of physical evolution has been one of the greatest handicaps in modern life. For it has had the effect of discounting the reality of man's spiritual nature and has intensified the horror of death. How can anyone be truly happy or willingly unselfish if he believes that death ends all? And so long as the majority are convinced that the life of the senses is the only reality we shall be unable to establish scientifically the fact of *post-mortem* existence. Can a man who has passed all his life in a blind dungeon prove that there is a sun? And he certainly will not be able to go further and explain how and why his very existence in the dungeon is dependent in a thousand ways upon the sun's invisible but all-sustaining life.

We must come out of the imprisoning dungeons of materialistic religion and science into the sunlight of spiritual Truth. Then we shall see that the real, inner man—the essential core of each of us—has always existed, is immortal at the present moment, and can no more be destroyed than can the boundless Universe of which it is an inseparable part.

Then, too, some satisfactory explanation must exist as to the prevailing injustices of life. There is hardly anyone who does not feel that life has more or less cheated him. Are not most of us born with desires and capacities that we shall never in this life have the opportunity to develop? And there are many indeed who are born with innate tendencies to evil which they are given no chance to outgrow. The glaring inequalities of modern life are in themselves enough to embitter the human heart and wither its moral initiative.

What is needed first of all is to demonstrate to man his significance in the evolutionary plan. We need a larger view of the purpose and destiny of the human race. Theosophy relates man to the Universe and shows that his individual consciousness is a ray of the Universal Cosmic Consciousness. It starts out by emphasizing that man is essentially a *center of consciousness*—not just a body to which a so-called soul is suddenly added at birth or death. Nor are we accidental products of blind, mechanical forces. Each individual is part of a living, organic Universe. That Universe itself is a product of evolution and carries forward within its own unfolding plan all that is—atoms, men, nebulae, worlds, solar systems, galaxies—in a grand sweep of development in which the humblest earthworm as certainly as the most godlike genius has a definite part.

The history of generations of oak-trees lies in the tiny acorn. From the heart of the acorn there slowly unfolds in response to Nature's influences a mighty tree which is an expression of an immense past of evolutionary oak-tree experience. So with the human being, the 'Man-plant of the Ages.' In that divine unit of consciousness which is the inner source of our individual life is stored the essence of an immense past stretching backward across immemorial ages. And our appearance as man on this earth is but one act in the magnificent drama of our evolution.

Nor is the human race itself a recent development of Nature. Man came from former cycles of evolution and resumed a body here on Earth, which is his present training-school. Further, there has not been constant 'creation' of new souls all down the ages. The number of evolving human beings on this Earth, though immense, is yet fixed and constant. This means that, in line with the economy of Nature, men as evolving Egos have been reborn on Earth again and again. All of us who make up our present civilization have been here many times before. We were the men and women who formed the great civilizations of the past, and we have also been imbodied in the many magnificent prehistoric races which Theosophy tells us something about.

Theosophy, therefore, begins with pre-existence as a necessary part of eternity. For a thing which has a beginning must necessarily come to an end. Nature makes that plain enough. What we call eternity or 'immortality' must stretch endlessly back into the past as well as endlessly forward into the future. The innermost Self of man is a deathless Being, a god, which reclothes itself from age to age in new bodies, or vehicles, that it may undergo all possible experiences in the Universe to which it belongs, and so reach its own most complete growth and self-expression.

Rebirth is the pathway of evolution. It is the method by which Nature progressively draws into growth or unfoldment the limitless capacities latent in all creatures from atoms to gods. Everything that has life reimbodies itself— universes, solar systems, suns, worlds; men, animals, and plants; cells, molecules, atoms. Each of these forms is ensouled by a spiritual consciousness-center which is evolving in its own degree, passing ever upward, and unfolding like a seed from within itself its latent potentialities.

In the human race we call this process of rebirth or reimbodiment by the word *Reincarnation,* which means 'refleshing,' or taking on again a garment or body of flesh. There are various names for the different forms of reimbodiment which pertain to all beings from the highest to the lowest, but here we are concerned only with that form of reimbodiment which pertains to man, and which is called reincarnation.

Human life is thus seen as a necessary and highly important part of the Cosmic Evolutionary Scheme. And we naturally inquire what its purpose is, for there seems to be no clear indication in the present confusion of beliefs and theories as to why we are here and what it is all for.

Briefly, the purpose of life is to raise the mortal into immortality. Or, to expand the idea somewhat, it is to give time and opportunity for the deathless spiritual potency at the core of man's being to develop, grow, unfold, into perfection. For Theosophy tells us that the personal man—the everyday self—is not immortal. John Smith and Mary Brown are not deathless beings. They are mere personalities, and as such do not reincarnate. It is the units of consciousness behind John Smith and Mary Brown, of which these perhaps quite ordinary persons are but the imperfect aspects—this root of consciousness in each, this Ego it is which reincarnates.

What man or woman has not often felt how short life is—how inadequate to express all that one feels of inspiration and capacity within his nature? How often we hear it said: "I am only just learning to live—now when I am old and just about to die." The Universe, however, is not run in that cruelly wasteful fashion. The very fact that we intuitively *know* that there are large reserves of power and possibility within us seeking expression—the fact that nearly everyone yearns to develop, *to be*, that Greater Self which he senses within—this very urge to a larger and fuller life, is our daily witness to Nature's true purpose for man. It is only because we are so preoccupied with our limited, everyday consciousness as John Smith or Mary Brown, and live only at rare moments in that deep, divine urge of the greater being within, that we are for the most part unconscious of the larger possibilities of life for us.

Let a man, then, first of all try to realize that he is in his inmost nature a divine consciousness or Ego; that this Ego which is himself has always existed, and shall never cease to live and grow, and develop toward perfection. Let him set his desire and will to realize his oneness with this divine Ego and to bring it out in his daily life as a larger, deeper individuality than that of his personal consciousness. He will then enter upon a new life. He will become a creator, a self-generator of his own illimitable divine destiny. He will begin at last to work self-consciously with the real purpose of evolution.

It is through reincarnation alone that man can bring out, and use, and perfect, the fullness of that hidden wealth of power and capacity of which we are all conscious in some measure. For through reincarnation the Ego undergoes every kind of human experience which this earth affords. In each life some new facet of character is shaped by environment. New powers and capacities are unfolded from within. Weaknesses, selfishness, and the faults of passion are corrected by suffering, that wise teacher which enables us to recognize and overcome our egoism and limitations.

Every new life gives us another chance. The criminal thus has time and opportunity to reform *himself,* and through restitution and self-mastery can advance to better things. One whose need to support and work for others all his life has made cultivation of his musical or other gifts impossible will, by the very strength of that dammed back energy and the moral power generated by devotion to duty, find increased capacity with freedom in another life for its development. So if we use well our opportunities we shall grow steadily from life to life until in some future reincarnation on this Earth character will flower into divine genius and we shall live and work in the fullness of our true spiritual being.

It is necessary to distinguish between Individuality and the personality; for, though these words may be used indiscriminately in common parlance, we must give them special meanings in speaking of Reincarnation. The Individuality is that which persists; the personalities are peculiar to the successive incarnations, and are not permanent as such. They are the growth which springs up after each birth on earth. Our personality changes greatly during a lifetime, but within it is the kernal of identity, and the faculty of memory binds it together. But dissolution brings about a major change and severs the links of memory. The separate beads of the string are disconnected; it is only the string which is continuous throughout. The memory of past incarnations inheres in the thread-soul.

—Henry T. Edge
"Thoughts on Reincarnation"

II

WHAT IT IS IN MAN
THAT REINCARNATES

SO far as we have gone we discover that man is a composite being. We have already observed three elements in his constitution: a personality known to friends as John Smith or Mary Brown, and back of that a deeper reservoir of consciousness expressed in the ideal desires of the nature. Lowest of all there is the animal consciousness, including the body, the vehicle of these two higher aspects in human life.

These three elements can still further be resolved until we see man as a sevenfold being. But in restricting our study now to the subject of reincarnation it will be necessary to regard him only in the threefold division above indicated. This corresponds to St. Paul's description of man as body, soul, and spirit. Christian theologians, however, have persistently ignored this division because they have no conception of the nature of Spirit. In making this threefold division St. Paul proved himself familiar with the teachings of the Ancient Wisdom, today known as Theosophy.

It is the higher, ideal nature above referred to which reincarnates. The technical name used in Theosophy for this higher part of our consciousness is *Manas*. This is a Sanskrit word

and means 'the thinker,' so we may call the
Reincarnating Ego the Thinker in man. It is the
origin of our *self*-consciousness, of the faculty
of introspection, and of self-realization. Through
it we relate ourselves to life, understand what
we are learning, and so build into ourselves in
the shape of character and propensities the
lessons derived from evolution. Without this
center of permanent individual consciousness
in which the results of evolution can be
preserved, the fruit of experience would be
dissipated at death and no progressive evolution would be possible. Through this spiritual
part of us comes also the voice of conscience.
From it we draw high inspiration, unselfish
love, intimations and intuitions of the divine,
and all impulses to impersonal, magnanimous
thought and action.

Thus two selves exist within us: the Self of
the Ego, or Thinker, which persists through all
our reincarnations; and the self of the personality, which is mortal and breaks up at death. It
is the play of consciousness between these two
which is the great mystery of life. Both of these
selves, as yet contradictory in desire and
purpose, make us what we are. How familiar
everyone is with the duel between them, which
is constantly going forward within us! The
voice of selfish temptation and the call of
incorruptible conscience—each striving against
the other for mastery. The struggle is of a
depth and complexity unsuspected until we
start out in earnest to conquer some habitual

fault, like a bad temper, or a weakness of some kind, or an ingrained selfishness. How quickly then we find all the forces within and without us arrayed either on one side or the other! The victory in such deep-seated, essential strife as this between the two natures of man, is far too many-sided and involves too wide a range of influences to be completely secured in one short life of limited experience. The struggle must be met under myriad conditions and attained by means of many experiences in life after life until at last complete mastery remains with the higher nature.

What is the origin of this duality within us? Why should man be both noble and ignoble? Theosophy describes how the external, animal vehicle of man was built up in long past ages of evolution on our globe by the lower, instinctual forces of Nature. Slowly it was shaped under the action of evolutionary law as a vehicle for the Reincarnating Ego. When this vehicle of body and animal consciousness was ready, the Spiritual Ego took it in charge, incarnating there to overshadow and guide its further development. The presence of the Ego now began dynamically to change, to mold, this vehicle for experience in human life. The spiritual fire of the Thinker through life after life stimulated and developed the growth of the animal man, so that gradually it unfolded or evolved under this creative influence a semi-independent personal consciousness of its own. And this personal consciousness, expanding slowly, slowly through ages of incarnation under the inspiration of its overshadowing Ego, became the human personality. And now not only is it an instrument through which the Ego may manifest its own divine powers, but gradually by its own struggles and victories under the urge of conscience—the personality itself is evolving. It unfolds and expands, and rising out of the limited personal consciousness, achieves thereby its own immortality. By subjecting our lower selfish natures to the influence and guidance of the higher we enable the Ego to express its light on this plane and thus exercise and expand its own divine potencies. On the other hand, gradually raising our personal consciousness, we lift it at last onto the plane of the Spiritual Ego, and so the human is transmuted into the immortal man. Thus the whole nature in all its elements has passed upward into a more advanced stage of consciousness. A graphic statement of this lifting of the whole being in all its parts is thus given by Dr. G. de Purucker:

> The work of evolution is . . . the raising of the personal into the Impersonal; the raising of the mortal to put on the garments of Immortality; the raising of the beast to become a man; the raising of a man to become a god; and the raising of a god to become still more largely divine.
> *Fundamentals of the Esoteric Philosophy,* p. 287

But indeed, the personal part of us is only on the evolutionary road to such perfection. We are yet far from the goal. The whole race is held in the grip of its ignorance of the spiritual, in the grip of suffering and confusion of mind and heart, because we have not yet learned to center our consciousness in the permanent and real part of us—the Spiritual Ego. We are immersed almost altogether in the personal interests of our nature. And this personality is mixed, a mentality, combined with passion, with emotional qualities, with physical traits and appetites. At different times any one of these may hold the mastery. At one moment the individual may be calculating with keen and absorbed mind, at another time swept from his moorings by a gust of violent anger. Again, physical pain or illness may turn him into a creature of ailing impotence. But seldom is any one of us for long the same. We pass from mood to mood and our outlook on life changes perpetually and is never stable. And like all composite things this unstable personality must break up when the time comes for the dissolution of the different energies and classes of life-atoms of which it is composed. For only homogeneous natures are immortal.

This bundle of personal energies, when it is broken up at the withdrawal of the Spiritual Ego into its own sphere, in other words at death—leaves behind it what in Theosophy are called *skandhas*. When a plant withers and dies, it drops into the earth the seeds which are the fruit of its little round of growth and development. From these seeds other plants will grow up when the cycle of the seasons has brought back the conditions necessary for their germination. If it was a fragrant violet, its seeds will produce their lovely kind. If it was a ragweed, more ragweeds will appear. So with the psychological-animal organism of man. When it dies and fades out it deposits in Nature's psychological soil or reservoir those invisible seeds of energy which its own growth has produced. Theosophists call these seeds or effects *skandhas,* using the Sanskrit because there is in English no word which can exactly describe these inner consequences of a life's experience. And it is these seeds or *skandhas,* or attributes of character, which shape the new personality when the Ego returns to incarnation, making it the exact result of what it thought and acted and built up of character in the last life.

That in man which reincarnates, then, is the Spiritual Ego, the higher part of our human constitution.

It has often been asked why we do not remember our past incarnations. To answer this, we must first distinguish between *memory* and *recollection*. Memory is the stored-up record of experiences, and recollection is the bringing back of memories into our present consciousness. Hence the memory of our past lives may be all stored up in some part of our nature, and yet we may be incapable of bringing it back to recollection. This incapacity, however, is not to be wondered at. The experiences of our last life took place in an entirely different *body,* with a different *brain.* They were not carried over as *conscious* recollections into this life at all; and upon the page of our infantile brain-mind were speedily written the gathered experiences pertaining to our present life.

—Henry T. Edge
"Facts and Fancies About
Reincarnation"

III
WHY DO WE NOT REMEMBER
OUR PAST LIVES?

T HE fact is that we *do* remember them. The question is here put in this form because that is how it is generally asked by inquirers. But it is not thus correctly phrased. It should rather be: "Why are we not able to recall the circumstances of our past lives?" For character itself is memory. In a certain family are born two children. One is candid and honorable, the other thieving and sly, and the second has to be painfully disciplined into a sense of honor. We all know of these puzzling cases of differing character in one family. The first has learned by experience in past incarnations that dishonesty is base, and so it is born with that innate knowledge as part of its character. The other child has this victory yet to achieve, and will the better achieve it because of its family environment—a favorable condition earned by the beginning of effort toward learning this lesson in a previous incarnation. It is in this way that we can say that character is memory.

Genius too is memory. All inborn faculties, whether good or evil, are the consequences of past self-training or of past weakness in other lives on earth. Mercifully, it is rare that anyone can remember the particular events through which these victories or failures as to character and faculty have been built into the inner nature. For since we learn almost always through suffering and many initial failures, such memories would in the main be of a painful kind.

We might also include hereditary traits as a phase of memory, developing a little more fully the subject above alluded to. Why is it for example that of three children born into the same family, one is a genius, another has a shrewd business head, while the third is entirely commonplace? Theosophy teaches that an Ego coming to birth must automatically, by the natural attraction of psychomagnetic energy, imbody those hereditary qualities and traits appropriate to the expression of its own nature brought over from its experience and actions in the past life. We thus see that in every way character is memory. And without these stored-up, accumulated memories, carried over from life to life—as before emphasized—no evolution of organism either physical, mental, or moral would be possible. Evolution depends upon continuity. Moreover, everything repeats itself. It is the method of Nature that through repetition characteristics are fixed and the type developed. Likewise is it by repetition through life after life that lessons of human character are realized and absorbed and become a permanent part of man's nature.

What is true of brain-memory is also true of

the personality. As indicated in Chapter I, the Ego has a different personality with each life. This must of necessity be so because in each life we learn something new, develop mentally and morally, unfold emotionally or spiritually, so that the old personality becomes inadequate— the Ego outgrows its possibilities as an instrument. The Ego, therefore, when it is reborn, makes for itself a fresh personality fashioned from the lessons incorporated into itself in the last life. For the personality is not the real I, it is only the mask, or vehicle, or garment, or temporary character through which the real I expresses an aspect of itself. Then consider the structure of the brain. Though the same atoms which made up the brain in a former life are now used again by the reincarnating entity, the brain of the new personality is a fresh combination entirely. For these life-atoms themselves have undergone changes (as explained in Chapter IV) so that while the instinctive trend is the same the total effect is a fresh outlook in the character.

So here is another and deeper reason why memories inhere and persist but details are forgotten, when the Ego returns to incarnation. Characteristics, faculties, which were built into the inner nature are brought back as unconscious memories; but the new-born personality, through the working of nature's compassionate laws, has no recollection of the actual happenings of a former life.

Another reason, and a basic one, why men do

not remember the circumstances of past lives is that the Universe to which we belong is an expression of intelligence, wisdom, and compassion. It is an organism, an immense, interblended series of infinitely graded living entities, having at its center or heart a Divine Intelligence, one of the Cosmic Gods. The 'laws' of the Universe are the life-rhythms—spiritual, intellectual, and vital—of that Cosmic Divinity, flowing out along the Circulations of the Cosmos, guiding and controlling all things from the mighty Sun to the electrons of the atom.

These beneficent laws protect man, as far as his free will does not prevent, against those things which hinder his evolution. Evolution always looks forward, is constructive, builds afresh and on developing patterns. Foremost among hindrances to evolution would be a constant preoccupation with the past. Man is supplied by the laws of the Cosmos with an adequate memory of his own past and that of the race, all that he needs to use: he is protected in the very nature of things from a memory of details which would burden, distract, and bring suffering to his upward struggling nature. To leave behind the low-vaulted past is one of the conditions of growth. Does the oak bother about the acorn which produced it, or the butterfly take thought for its abandoned chrysalis? We are children of a Universe of Life, and we are forever and healthily abandoning the worn-out and developing the new out of the old.

All of us undoubtedly, as Spiritual Egos, have played many parts on this wonderful stage of the human drama, our planet Earth. It is through these manifold roles that we have developed the highly complex psychological apparatus called human nature, which in the great majority is able to adjust itself to almost any condition of human existence, under all climes and in any environment. So true is this that there is a great restlessness upon men today, a feeling that life as we know it has been lived out, exhausted of its possibilities. Mankind inarticulately feels itself upon the threshold of some new discovery. Theosophy proclaims that this is a genuine intuition, a prevision of the New Era which is just about to dawn upon the world.

We must not forget, however, that a time will eventually come when each of us will be able clearly to recollect all the events of our past lives. The register of everything that has ever happened to an individual is imprinted imperishably upon the deathless, divine side of his nature. But we have not yet developed the spiritual faculties which would enable us to read that mystic record. Nor shall we develop them so long as we constantly identify ourselves only with the life of the brain and the personality. For now self-interest shuts us in, passions hold us in selfish blindness, prejudice weaves its dense web over intuition and creative power. And so we languish in our narrow prisons of personality. Only occasionally, when the sunshine of divine love or the spirit of self-sacrifice inspires us, do we catch a gleam of the mountains of dawn without our prison walls. Man must use his spiritual will to realize his essential godhood and break through the bonds of selfishness and ignorance into the glorious kingdom lying just beyond the threshold of his everyday consciousness.

For logic, consistency, profound philosophy, divine mercy and equity, this doctrine of Reincarnation has not its equal on earth. It is a belief in a perpetual progress from the outward into the inward, from the material to the Spiritual, arriving at the end of each stage at absolute unity with the divine Principle. From strength to strength, from the beauty and perfection of one plane to the greater beauty and perfection of another, with accessions of new glory, of fresh knowledge and power in each cycle, such is the destiny of every Ego, which thus becomes its own Savior in each world and incarnation.

—H. P. Blavatsky
The Key to Theosophy

IV

SOME OBJECTIONS AND MISCONCEPTIONS

ONE of the commonest mistakes made by inquirers is the belief that reincarnation means that a man can be reborn in the body of an animal. Some Oriental religions teach that such animal-incarnation is a punishment for certain sins. This doctrine is a distortion, which came about in the course of centuries, of an original teaching to be explained later. Theosophy denies this doctrine emphatically; all its teachings are a refutation of this idea. "Once a man, always a man" is one of the great axioms of the Archaic Science. This statement is based on the fact, already referred to, that the Universe is a living organism. We are a part of that great organism and the laws therefore which govern our life spring from the nature of that organism. Thus by understanding what happens in the physical world we can get an idea of the corresponding processes in all other spheres or planes within the boundaries of our own Universe.

Looking at man from this standpoint we see that as the circulations of the human being, arterial and nervous, make growth possible, so do the universal circulations, vital and spiritual, make evolution possible. In man the life forces flow along definite channels called veins, arteries, and nerves. In the Universe the evolutionary pulsations also pass along definite channels and are called in Theosophy the Circulations of the Cosmos. The relation of this fact to the permanence of the Ego as a human being has been well expressed:

Manas the Thinker . . . does not return to baser forms; first, because he does not wish to, and second, because he cannot. For just as the blood in the body is prevented by valves from rushing back and engorging the heart, so in this greater system of universal circulation the door is shut behind the Thinker and prevents his retrocession. Reincarnation as a doctrine applying to the real man does not teach transmigration into the kingdoms of nature below the human.

—W. Q. Judge: *The Ocean of Theosophy*

This distortion of the law of Reincarnation referred to as "the transmigration of the soul" is a misapplication of a fact anciently known and now again brought forward by Theosophy—the transmigration of the life-atoms. In our literature it has been often explained, as in the following passage:

In the application of this word to the life-atoms . . . it means, briefly, that the life-atoms which in their aggregate compose man's lower principles, at and following the change that men call death, migrate or transmigrate or pass into other bodies to which these life-atoms are psycho-magnetically attracted, be these attractions high or low—and they are usually low, because their own evolutionary development is as a rule far from being advanced.

—G. de Purucker: *The Esoteric Tradition*, p. 598

If a man has led a grossly animal existence the life-atoms of which the cells of his body are composed will automatically through attraction pass into those bodies or substances which will afford the appropriate outlet for the kind of energy which has been built into them. If the life of another has been high and fine the vibrations impressed upon the atoms will cause them to be attracted only to clean, wholesome, finely organized substances or organisms. When the period of rebirth comes again, and the life-atoms return by the action of psychomagnetic attraction to the reincarnating entity to which they belong, they bring with them a reinforcement—through their transmigrations—of the bad or good influences educated into them during the last life. Thus it is easy to see how this teaching of the transmigrations of the life-atoms has, like so many of the occult doctrines, been degraded by ignorance of priestcraft from its original and true significance.

A good many object to reincarnation because they do not like the idea of coming back to this earth. They feel that they have had enough of the sorrows and difficulties of human life and do not wish to return to it. And such an objection is just as natural and understandable as a child's objection to being kept in school. But not for nothing has the term 'Mother Nature' been a universal one in all ages, for it springs from man's instinctive knowledge that we are her children, that she is greater and wiser than we are, and will hold us to her laws of evolution and discipline whether we will or no. No man by merely taking thought can add one cubit to his stature or change any of the processes of life or death. It may be said that the truth of reincarnation cannot be proved. But it is so grounded in probabilities as founded on all the ways of Nature—day and night, life and death, sleeping and waking, summer and winter, the phases of all planetary motion, and the very cycles of the sun itself; it is so natural and instinctive a human belief, being at the present time the conviction of a large majority of the human race, and in olden times always universally accepted; it makes such a strong appeal to man's heart and logic that thousands upon hearing it for the first time have accepted it at once as an inevitable conclusion from the facts of life. Moreover, it is at the present time spreading rapidly among all classes of thinking men; and it is seen to have such power to reform and satisfy and inspire human nature, that it must, once encountered, become a theory that can at least never again be forgotten or ignored.

These things are but a part of the overwhelming 'presumptive evidence' for reincarnation. To deny it, to say, "I do not want to come back to earth," is hardly enough. There is a general tendency in human nature to adopt the easiest way, to think that because we find a certain course unpleasant and another one more agreeable we must be allowed to please ourselves. And this in spite of the fact that the very sorrows and difficulties we are so tired of are there to convince us to the contrary. Man must somewhere meet the consequences of his thoughts and actions, his failures and moral victories. Why not here—here on this earth, where he can reap the harvest on the spot where the seed was sown?

Let us remember, however, that these teachings of Theosophy have nothing to do with what is called fatalism. We are indeed held in the grip of our present circumstances, because having intertwined ourselves by former actions into these circumstances we cannot escape them until by a reverse course of action we effect our own liberation. But at any moment that anyone can see and admit that he has this power, and then sets about using his will, he begins to be a master of those circumstances and can use them to bring about exactly contrary results to what they would have produced if he had tamely submitted to them. Thus man, using knowledge and free will, becomes increasingly master of himself and therefore of his destiny. Theosophy is foremost among all systems of thought in arousing us to this knowledge and realization of our power, and so leading us into creative progress and freedom.

Again people sometimes say, "But if we are all reborn into different bodies how shall I know my friends?" Theosophy answers that no act of recognition is necessary. We and our present family and friends are knitted together by love, by mutual experience, and by congeniality. We shall not have to seek each other out. Families will be reborn together in continuation of the bonds they are united by now. We and our friends can no more help being attracted and brought together than a magnet can help selecting iron filings from surrounding soil. We cannot escape our friends, or—it must also be emphasized—our enemies!

And there are not a few who object to the idea of being reborn as an infant and having to learn all over again the merely physical side of existence, as well as repeating in each life elementary education and brain-development. But, as has been pointed out before, this repetition of even physical experience is a habit of Nature that has been essential to evolution.

We are assured that eventually, in the long course of evolution, as man's spiritual development proceeds, he will grow out of the need for this form of repetition.

The whole point for us lies of course in the influence of *spiritual* development. We are burdened by conditions of physical weakness because in the past we have bound ourselves into slavery to them, by living, thinking, and longing nearly altogether for material and personal satisfactions. These, being self-centered or centripetal in action, create bonds which hinder the spiritual progress of the Reincarnating Ego. So the need is to so spiritualize and impersonalize ourselves that all limitations and weaknesses will gradually dissolve away. The Ego will then be free to control and develop its vehicles of self-expression in harmony with its own divine nature and purposes.

Objections to reincarnation spring as a rule from unfamiliarity with the teaching and its innumerable close applications to the problems and situations arising in life. And there are, naturally, some who will not accept it because they do not wish to believe it. But the great majority who encounter this doctrine are almost sure, sooner or later, to join that growing multitude of all kinds and classes of people—not by any means all of whom profess Theosophy—to whom reincarnation is the very foundation of human justice, happiness, and spiritual growth.

All these souls, when they have completed
the circle of the revolving years, the god
summons in long array to Lethe's stream, so
that losing remembrance of the past they may
again enter the vaulted arch above, and then
begin to feel desire to re-enter mortal bodies.

—Virgil
Aeneid, vi. 746-751

V

THE PROCESSES OF REINCARNATION

GRANTING that reincarnation is true, where was I before I was born? This is a question pretty sure to follow in the wake of the foregoing discussion. So far we have said little about death, one of the grandest and most important processes of life; nor shall we now go deeply into it for it is discussed fully in the manual *After Death–What?*

As said before, man is, broadly speaking, a threefold entity, and those three basic elements in his constitution give him a triple line of evolution: the spiritual, the mental-emotional, and the astral-vital; and the physical body is the channel through which these express themselves.

When the body dies and breaks up, dissipating its astral-vital energies, the process is followed by the gradual dissolution of the whole personality, the mental-emotional being. Yet there will still be something, in some cases a very large part, of the personality which endures. The Spiritual Ego will absorb into itself all the personality that it can, that part of it

39

which is of its own nature—its spiritual
aspirations, its true and abiding loves, its
unselfish and pure desires. Whatever is spiritual in man partakes of the Universal Divine
which animates and supports the Cosmos. An
ideal of unselfishness, purity, and noble
actions, consistently lived up to, transmutes the
personal elements which strive and aspire into
the incorruptible gold of spirit. It raises the
mortal into immortality. When death comes
this transmuted energy is not dissipated; it is
incorporated into its own nature by the
Reincarnating Ego.

This incorporation is assisted by the very
mystical experience which takes place at the
time of death. In that solemn and beautiful
hour after the last sigh has been given, the Ego
hovers for a brief time upon the threshold of
the earthly portal. And then, before its now
unclouded vision, there passes a panorama,
like the unwinding of a living scroll, of all that
has happened, down to the least detail from
birth to death in the life just ended. In its
dawning freedom the self-conscious Thinker
follows these life-scenes and can then see the
plan and significance of all its experiences, the
relation of the parts to the whole, and of this
life to those gone before. The justice, the
necessity, and the beneficence of its trials and
sufferings, with their guerdon of wisdom, are
brought home to the egoic consciousness.
These memories are now carried with it as it
ascends into the Heaven-world, called in

Theosophy *Devachan*. Here it passes a long period of blissful rest. Is this not one aspect of what Jesus meant when he said, "Lay up for yourself treasures in Heaven where neither moth nor rust doth corrupt"?

This spiritual rest in the inner Heaven-world gives the reincarnating entity an opportunity to absorb and assimilate the experiences of its last life on earth. For the same rhythmic cycle of activity—sleep, rest, assimilation, followed by refreshed energies—characterizes not only our physical bodies, but is experienced by all living entities, whether physical, psychological, or spiritual. And, correspondingly, it applies also to atomic, planetary, stellar, and cosmic organisms.

It may prove clarifying to review the chief reasons why the Ego in man, the Thinker, is awakened out of his blissful term of happiness to return to the tasks, the joys and sorrows, of another life on earth. The first of these reasons is that man and all things in Nature follow a universal pattern: birth, growth, youth, maturity, decline, death—and rebirth.

The second and a most compelling reason is the thirst for material life: the hunger, the yearning for the scenes and experiences of a past to which we consciously or unconsciously cling.

But there are those, as noted before, who vehemently declare: "I don't *want* to come back back to this earth! I want to go somewhere else where I can forget it all and never think of this world again!" But is this verily so? For those of us who have lost a beloved helpmate or child, must not that 'somewhere else' include those loved forms exactly as we remember them? Our regrets for past mistakes or unkindnesses, a lifelong dream of a career that was never possible, unsatisfied longings for books, music, travel, luxuries, congenial friends, or for the power to help others—these are indeed energies: somewhere they must work out into their due consequences. These desires make the unconscious hunger of the human heart, and only human life can satisfy them. And they may well be called 'secret causes' because we are so unaware of them as formative energies.

The following will give us the metaphysical side of the matter:

This 'thirst' is a composite instinctual habit, compounded of a host of things—as all habits are, if we analyze ourselves—of loves, hates, affections of various kinds, magnetic attractions of the hosts of life-atoms composing man's constitution, both visible and invisible, and of longings and yearnings of many types, all of which collect during the various life-terms on earth into the human soul and mind, and which for these reasons are called by Theosophists 'thought-deposits'—emotional and mental and psychic tendencies and biases. All these are energies, . . . and they will energize the reincarnating entity's destiny until evolution and expanding consciousness and the purification of suffering finally transfer man's consciousness as an individual being to higher planes. . . .

—G. de Purucker: The *Esoteric Tradition*, p. 874

Then there is the other side of the picture—the pull of the life-atoms. This is yet a third cause for the return of the Ego to earth-incarnation.

> . . . it [the Reimbodying Ego] 'descends' through the same intermediate planes or worlds by which it had previously ascended at the end of the preceding earth-life, and it takes up again as many as possible of those very life-atoms which had been left there during the previous ascent and which are now drawn back again to the descending Reimbodying Ego because of affinity. . . .
>
> —*Op. cit.,* p. 790

These life-atoms do not all belong to the physical plane. There are different classes or grades of them acting in the three general planes of evolution already referred to—the physical, mental-emotional, and the spiritual. Each of these classes of life-atoms manifests a degree of evolution corresponding to the plane in which it belongs. Life-atoms are infinitesimal, undeveloped god-sparks emanated by the central Life-Flame at the Heart of our Universe, and they are the building blocks on all planes of the Cosmos: they form the 'stuff' of which are built the three planes of evolution just spoken of, and from which the higher beings on that plane fashion their vehicles and are thus able to manifest and express themselves therein. Thus man expresses bodily actions and functions by means of the life-atoms which make up his body until death occurs and liberates them to pursue their transmigrations. Likewise he has his mental-emotional and also his spiritual life-atoms through which his personal and Ego-life express themselves. In thinking of these mental-emotional life-atoms as awaiting the reincarnating entity we must remember where they have been since the Ego passed out of earth-life through the portal of death:

> . . . these life-atoms of man's intermediate nature, in other words of his vehicular 'soul,' are freed from the overlordship of the Monadic Ray and form a host or group or multitude on interior planes; and all these multitudes of various kinds or classes of life-atoms are attracted to or seek refuge as it were in other human beings. . .
>
> —*Op. cit.,* p. 782

There are of course other causes which contribute to the Ego's irresistible urge to return to earth-life, but here we have said enough to indicate the underlying 'laws,' or 'habits' of nature.

We come now to the process by which the Ego re-enters existence upon this planet Terra. Owing to the causes mentioned above, combined with others equally compelling, the Reincarnating Ego at last awakens out of its blissful heaven-dream and begins its 'descent' earthwards. Its progress is very gradual. Not much is told in the exoteric teachings of Theosophy as to the various states of substance and consciousness through which the Ego passes in its approach to the threshold of material life. But we know of course that at first these states are psychological, as the Ego is *Manas,* the thinking-principle, the creative, formative, self-conscious intellectual element in us. This psychological element combines with the emotional to make the personality which is the distinctive 'human' consciousness in man. Thus the psychological-emotional life-atoms awaiting the Ego on the threshold of rebirth, are used to make the first garment or vehicle which the Ego weaves around itself as it emerges from the higher spiritual realms. Then the lower vital forces come into play—the life-atoms of ethereal or astral and physical substance guided by their formative tendencies ingrained into them in the last life, and further strengthened in these by their transmigrations during the interhuman interval.

It is the life-atoms which carry the *skandhas* referred to in Chapter II. As already said, the life-atoms are, during their association with the reincarnated entity, impressed or imprinted or shaped with the physical, emotional, and mental trends of the life being lived. What their own transmigrations are after the dissolution of the body at death will be influenced by these *skandhas,* or attributes of character. And when the life-atoms return to the entity about to reincarnate it is these *skandhas* imbodied so to say in the life-atoms that will furnish the nature and characteristics of the mental, emotional, and physical vestures of its new earth-life.

Again, referring to the process of birth itself we are told:

> . . . the reincarnating entity, now rebecomes a bundle or aggregate of substance, is . . . drawn magnetically and psychically to the family or to the particular human womb where vibrational conditions most similar to its own exist.

Its lowest, i.e., more material, force and substance connect psycho-magnetically through its own astral-vital
fluid with the 'laya-center' of a human generative particle
when the appropriate time comes; and from the instant of
conception, 'the appropriate time,' the reincarnating entity 'overshadows' that particle as this particle grows from
conception through its different phases of intra-uterine
life, birth, childhood, into full adulthood.

—*Op. cit.,* p. 893

Here we naturally encounter popular
theories of heredity, which nowadays is sup-
posed to be the determining cause of all our
characteristics of mind and body. Heredity,
however, simply pushes a little further back,
without explaining, inequalities in human destiny. Why are some men born in the slums and
others with every possible advantage? It is such
facts as these that do more to discourage the
average man than anything else, and they cry
out for an explanation.

But when we remember the selective
—because psycho-magnetic—qualities of the
various psychological, emotional, astral, and
vital sheaths, garments or vehicles, already,
even before conception, formed around the
Ego, we see that a reincarnating entity im-
bodies automatically from its family stream of
heredity exactly those tendencies which cor-
respond to its own nature developed in the
past. Thus viewed, our so-called heredity is
seen for what it actually is, only another name
for the effect of creative energies, high or low,
generated by the individual itself in its own
past. The family and the parents give but the
inevitable channel through which these self-

generated energies work themselves out as consequences in character, temperament, and physical constitution.

At this point we encounter another instance of Nature's creative processes of repetition. For, just as the Ego on leaving the body sees, as above described, a living picture of the just ended earth-life, so immediately before it reincarnates, is this process repeated. The events of the coming life are then all foreseen by the Being standing upon the threshold of human existence. The necessity and the justice of all that will happen in the coming life are accepted by the Reincarnating Ego, which then enters willingly upon a fresh attempt to guide and urge the human personality through conscience and love into the ways of self-knowledge and self-mastery.

It is interesting to remember that because our whole nature is made up of the life-atoms used by us in many past lives we are practically the same personality of our past life: yet, because all these life-atoms come together at birth in fresh combinations and after manifold new experiences of their own, in harmony with our own past, our new personality is in many respects different from the one we had grown so tired of when death kindly compelled us to lay it down like a worn-out tool.

Is it not wonderful to be forever the same, and yet forever new?—forever developing and changing and perfecting the consciousness-stuff and energy-stuff, and the matters of all grades through which and by means of which as spiritual Egos we work?

As to the length of the period between incarnations we may say this is usually about a hundred times the length of the life last lived on earth. There are exceptions, of course. The important thing to remember is that it is the quality of the life just lived, the sum and substance of character, that really controls both the experiences and the time-period in the after-death states. The more spiritual the life on earth the longer is the need for the rest and bliss of Devachan. This is more fully explained in the Manual on *After Death – What?*

This brief sketch may give some idea of the complex nature of the doctrine of Reincarnation. And yet, too, it is all so majestically simple when once the basic principles of evolution are grasped. These are: the unity of all beings; the cyclic and periodic nature of all manifested life; and the obligation of all entities—supernally high or elementally humble, which make up the Cosmos—to pass continually forward upon an ever ascending spiral of reimbodiment.

. . . thus, finding myself to exist in the world, I believe I shall, in some shape or other, always exist; and, with all the inconveniences human life is liable to, I shall not object to a new edition of mine, hoping, however, that the errata of the last may be corrected.

—Benjamin Franklin

VI

THE ETHICAL INFLUENCE OF A
BELIEF IN REINCARNATION

A survey of our world of today suggests that
the keynote of these times might be appro-
priately regarded as irresponsible indi-
vidualism. Anything, almost, which contri-
butes to the 'free development of personality'
would appear to be allowable. And the results,
as we see them recorded in the daily press or
meet them in our vain efforts at moral and
social reform, are deplorable.

We need a new basis for the ethical education
of the individual. Churches, educational in-
stitutions, social service measures, prison reform, all are useful: they serve to keep things
going. But until the individual *child* can be
trained from infancy to a rational, heart-
satisfying philosophy of life, growing out of the
facts of Nature itself, there will be no constructive, lasting improvement in the moral character of our civilization.

Such a rational and well-nigh irresistible
basis for education and living is offered in
Theosophy. Reincarnation is but one of the
many comprehensive and searching truths
which it contains. Every one of the laws it points

out anew to man is grounded in Nature, and evidence for the existence of these laws is drawn from our experiences of the life around us. There is no science or philosophy in the Western world today, outside of Theosophy, which can explain life itself or show an inevitable basis in Nature for morals and ethics. Theosophy, if one will study it conscientiously and fairly as one would study chemistry or music in the hope of mastering either, will solve our every problem. It will give a purpose to all living and an individual objective both satisfactory and inspiring.

Reincarnation—which, as already said, means the periodic rebirth of the Reincarnating ego as a human being on this earth until it has exhausted the earth's evolutionary possibilities for it—is but one aspect of the general law of reimbodiment. Reimbodiment itself is an expression of the universal rhythm of life —that 'law' or *habit* of cyclic progression in the Universe which we see manifested everywhere as ebb and flow, night and day, sleeping and waking, life and death, the rise and fall of the seasons, the birth, growth, and decay of nations.

Let us now examine what a belief in Reincarnation ethically implies. First of all it changes a man's idea of himself. Probably he will think first of his own past. He accepts the idea that he has lived many times and thus must have had a share, no matter how important or even how obscure it may have been, in building some of the great civilizations of Earth. This gives him a sense of spaciousness, of really being somebody, which our modern standardized living and the 'born in sin' teaching had almost crushed out of him. Perhaps he has lost faith in religion. But Theosophy will give him a deep, inner vision of the Heart of the Universe, that glorious Sun of Universal Being of which every creature is a ray in its inmost essence. He will come gradually to feel his oneness with this Universal Life; and so the religious instinct will be reborn in his heart and he will be consoled and uplifted by a sense of union with the Heart of Divinity.

Later he will look around at his environment in this new light, realizing now that it is just what he prepared for himself in a former life. And a feeling of creative moral energy is born. *Why not change it, better it, since he has the power?* Initiative springs up in him, and the beginning of a regenerated activity. Next, he will turn to his relationships: his friends and—his enemies. Who are these people? Mere casual attachments? Why, no; of course not. They are his associates of eternity! Even this man he so heartily dislikes—that is because he has disliked him before in past lives, and the dislike has been growing, till now it fairly darkens his pleasure in life. Is this to go on increasing through all his future lives, leading to what dark ending no one can divine? Thinking like this he will begin to see the matter as his own problem rather than one of environment, and nine men out of ten will put all their moral ingenuity into solving it. And he will enjoy working it out. It is quite likely that he will end in understanding and loving the one who is now a mere thorn in the flesh; and far from wishing to see the last of him he will be added to the number of those who are to pass onward and upward with him to the next stage of evolution.

Marriage appears, under the pressure of modern conditions, to be growing more complicated and difficult with every decade. There is a sense of impermanence about it. Young people have no teaching that shows them any way to connect sex-life with ethical law. Sex is one of the facts of human existence which seems always to have defied moral law; so much so that many who are really sound at heart have given up in despair before the contradictions involved in this problem. Nowhere else, perhaps, do we drift as helplessly as in this one relation.

But young people who accept reincarnation come to realize that sex inheres only in the impermanent and perishable part of them, the lower personality; and that happiness which is permanent, which lasts in its essentials for always, belongs to the divine, imperishable Reincarnating Ego. They will be led to test this teaching by study in history and biography, by observation in the lives of those around them; by trying it out in thought and action in their own difficulties. In doing this they will make wonderful discoveries concerning the more enduring aspects of companionship and love which, could they be assured to the youth of the world, would revolutionize society.

Of course, too, young people who believe that they have been together before in other lives and that their present difficulties are the outcome of mistakes in the past on earth; and that is they slide out of the situation now it will only be postponing the settlement —aggravated the next time by compound karmic interest—such young people will have the common sense instinct to tackle the problem at once and work it out to a happy ending. As for the harmonious marriages we need only observe that in all human relationships and all forms of enduring love, the teaching of reincarnation throws a yet more beautiful and sacred light upon the reality of any true partnership in the higher purposes of evolution. But to make marriage real the love upon which it is built must have its source in the spiritual nature. So it is seen that a belief in reincarnation, when truly studied and understood, puts an end to all drifting, which is such a prevailing moral weakness of today.

Then how differently do the parents who believe in reincarnation regard their children, from the usual parent, who either thinks that his children 'belong' to him or looks upon them merely as the chance-born product of animal evolution. For Theosophy brings into the home the beautiful light of the essential Divinity of man. The birth of a child in the home of those who so believe is not a mere 'occurrence'; it is a divine event. The being about to reincarnate is returning from the Heaven-world and brings the atmosphere of a holier and purer sphere into the lives of those to whom it is entrusted. Both mother and father share in one of the deepest and most sacred mysteries of life. So they will not only prepare themselves to give their children the highest possible vehicles for their re-entry into this earth-life, but they will undertake with joy that wider preparation for wise and sympathetic guidance of their children through their karmic problems inherited from their past incarnations, of which they are themselves such an important part. How much they can do for their children's and their own evolution in this spirit can easily be seen by the thoughtful inquirer. And one need not do much thinking to understand what such an attitude can mean in the lives of both parents and children. These ideas have been most wonderfully expressed by Katherine Tingley in *The Wine of Life:*

A home established on these lines would have within it indeed the Kingdom of Heaven. Storms might rage without: trials, poverty, struggles, tragedies, disappointments of all kinds, might assail its peace from without; but no matter how many or how great they might be, they could not daunt the builders of this home; who have within, heaven, reflected in a home-life which is the expression of the Higher Law. Their children would be born into the wonder of the new happiness with which its atmosphere would be filled. Before the birth of each, they would make preparation for it in much more than the ordinary sense. They married understandingly, this couple; with knowledge of the laws of life; they were companions, and not merely lovers. A child is born to them, but their states of mind were fashioning its character before it saw the light; the influence of all the harmony, peace, hope, courage which they have brought into their lives was preparing for it a larger, broader path than is common, and an environment fit for a soul to live in; so that it finds itself after birth not exiled in this world, but at once at home in its surroundings.

We understand, when looking into the fundamental laws from which reincarnation springs, that evolution is a moral—a spiritual, rather than a mere physical process. Physical evolution is but the outermost and least important side of the matter. Of what use ultimately, a healthy and beautiful body if used for evil ends? And how many invalids, and even people who are perhaps outwardly unattractive have contributed treasures of inspiration to the world's need! We have only to recall Socrates or Dante to see the fallacy of the popular point of view. It is indeed a well-known fact that physical perfection has never been necessary and seldom present in cases of moral and intellectual genius. On the other hand how frequently it happens that physical beauty is a source of misfortune or moral backsliding. Character is the spiritual fabric woven by evolution. It is the only thing we can take out of life when we go: it is what we bring back as our heritage from the past when we return to incarnation on earth.

The whole modern philosophy of eat, drink, and be merry, for tomorrow we die, has grown out of the loss of realization that we are imperishable spiritual beings in our innermost. Materialistic science has educated the present generation to regard themselves largely as highly developed offshoots of the ape-family. The demoralizing effect of this teaching found nothing in religion with the authority of life and nature back of it that could counteract its degenerative influence. That was one of the main reasons why the Mahâtmas started the Theosophical Society through H. P. Blavatsky when this materialistic influence was approaching its apex in the last century. Theosophy has been steadily at work now for a century. Not only its published teaching but its potent invisible thought-influence has united with the spiritual instincts of humanity to free us gradually from this nightmare reaction against the superstitions of the past.

Theosophy shows the true spiritual ideal of evolution and its practical working out in all sides of life—spiritual, intellectual, moral, and physical. In reincarnation the ethical side of evolution is seen to be paramount, for here justice, moral consequences, growth in spiritual power are the decisive influences. None can develop the best within himself unless he grows spiritually. A power gained through lives of effort and used merely for selfish gratification withers, for it will be checked in later lives by the effects in suffering and difficulties of environment consequent upon that very selfishness. And the teaching of reincarnation makes it clear that the best way to make genius and character permanent and divine is to consecrate them to the service of humanity. It is in such wise that the great Saviors of history have been able to sway the minds and hearts of whole races of men.

We must not leave this subject without noticing another important ethical effect of this belief, and that is in the lives of old people. The great majority look with dread upon the coming of old age for, to most, if it does not mean either feebleness or actual physical and mental deterioration, at least it entails being 'put upon the shelf.' But Theosophy shows why it is that old age should be a most important part of life, as the following helps us to understand:

> . . . the Reincarnating Ego or 'soul' is not really fully incarnated until some rather short time before the physical body dies; which means that there is a constant and unceasing possibility for physical, mental, and spiritual development almost to the time of the dissolution of the physical body. In other words . . . old age is not, as is sometimes foolishly supposed, incapable of learning, and merely a distressing period in human existence where all the best is past and the future holds no hope except the bliss of dying. The exact reverse of this is true, for, theoretically at least, up to a short time before physical dissolution a man *should* progress steadily in both spiritual and intellectual power and faculty.
>
> —G. de Purucker: *The Esoteric Tradition*, p. 894

These words bring indeed a new and heartening message for us all. The wise ancients recognized this truth in maintaining that young men were for action and the old for counsel. One of the tragedies of modern life is the disproportion between the roles of youth and even of middle age—but the truth of reincarnation as presented in the passage above restores the balance. This is yet another case where the teachings of Theosophy give back hope and dignity and happiness to discouraged humanity.

We must however not overlook the fact that to realize at its best this ideal for old age it is necessary to so live in harmony with the divine in youth and middle age that old age may be the perfect harvest of this earlier spiritual development. Yet even so, an aging man or woman, meeting Theosophy for the first time, will find the practice of its teachings a wonderful creative power to restore purpose and energy and stimulate spiritual advancement in the years that remain.

Above all else reincarnation demonstrates that Brotherhood is the great reality of the universe. It is the basic and the supreme fact of nature. It governs all things in both their essence and their evolution. The first of all the elementary propositions of the Ancient Wisdom, Theosophy, stresses this universal essential unity. The most fundamental error that can be made is to deny either directly in thought or word or indirectly in action this truth of the utter oneness in essence of all beings. It is, we might almost say, to deny the Divine Source in which we all live and move and have our being. In *The Secret Doctrine* H. P. Blavatsky has given us the foundation in spiritual Nature of this truth. She establishes

The fundamental unity of all souls with the Universal Oversoul . . . and the obligatory pilgrimage for every soul—a spark of the former—through the Cycle of Necessity, in accordance with Cyclic and Karmic Law. . . . The pivotal doctrine of the Esoteric Philosophy admits no privileges or special gifts in man, save those won by his own Ego through personal effort and merit throughout a long series of metempsychoses* and reincarnations.

—*The Secret Doctrine,* I: 17

We thus see that all creatures have the same origin in the Universal One Life. Man at present is working out the purpose of his evolution through the Cycle of Necessity called on this earth reincarnation. In these facts we see the basic equality of all beings in origin, growth, and destiny. For at the very heart of everyone, of whatever grade or degree of evolution, there dwells a god-spark, a beam of the Oversoul, or the Universal Life. In the kingdoms below man this god-spark burns with but a feeble, instinctual light. In man it has increased and thrown out a selfconscious ray which lights his path clearly when he will let it and makes of him a responsible moral being. In the Mahâtmas this god-spark has expanded into the light of semigodhood, self-conscious union with the One Life; and in those Beings beyond and above the Mahâtmas the spark has gloriously flamed out into pure godhood. So on and up the mighty Stairway of Being which mounts out of the reach of our present spiritual vision and disappears into the glory of the invisible worlds.

*Metempsychosis is a word of wider meaning than reincarnation. It refers to the reimbodiment of the Spiritual Ego in other spheres than that of earth—in the inner, spiritual worlds.

The most beautiful side of this teaching lies in the essential responsibility of the higher for those less evolved. The gods brood over all planes of being, shedding inspiration and life upon the whole. The Mahâtmas, their self-evolved servants, are first of all Helpers and Elder Brothers of humanity, and although they have graduated from human life and its lessons and might pass on to higher spheres of evolution if they wished, they choose to remain near humanity to foster its spiritual development, helping the gods in their protection and guidance of men. From time to time, as already said, the Mahâtmas send out Messengers to teach in a new form the ancient truths of the Universe which during the course of ages have become distorted or forgotten. H. P. Blavatsky was such a Messenger and the Theosophical Society is the channel through which the Ancient Wisdom, Theosophy, after having been lost to the Western world for almost twenty centuries, is again restored to mankind.

A further development of this aspect of Universal Brotherhood in connection with reincarnation lies in man's own individual responsibility to the kingdoms next beneath him in evolution. In reference to the constant change and flux among the atoms forming our bodies, and in their dissolution and transmigration after man's physical death, the following is related to the above idea:

Man's emanations thus build up the animal world; the animals feed on these life-atoms of many kinds; physical, vital, astral, mental, and what not. . . . These life-streams issuing from him give life and evolutionary impulse and characteristics to the entities of the kingdoms below the human, because these subhuman kingdoms are the evolved productions of the thoughts and vital emanations of the human race.

—Golden Precepts

Brotherhood, then, is not merely an ideal or just a sentiment, but is a living fact. And all of our collective miseries can be traced to ignorance that brotherhood actually is a law of our being. Not understanding this we are forever disturbing, by selfishness of all kinds, the harmonious development of ourselves and of the race. It is through reincarnation, checked and guided by karma and helped by our Elder Brothers and those above them, that humanity at last learns the supreme lesson of human evolution—that only through selflessness and impersonal love can man achieve freedom, happiness, and power.

The very thing which is now called the Christian religion, really was known to the ancients, nor was it wanting at any time from the beginning of the human race up to the time Christ came in the flesh; from which time the true religion, which has previously existed, began to be called Christian, and this in our days is the Christian religion, not as having been wanting in former times, but as having in later times received that name.

—*Augustini Opera,* I, 12

VII

REINCARNATION AS A
HISTORICAL BELIEF

I T is a fact surprising to nearly everyone in Western countries that reincarnation was taught practically universally over the earth at the time when Christ was born. But this is only because we have not been educated to associate this doctrine historically with the Jews or with the ancient Greeks and Romans. It is a still more surprising fact that it was accepted by some of the Church Fathers and prevailed so widely in early Christendom that, as late as the middle of the sixth century after Christ it was necessary to convene a special Church Council in order finally to suppress it. After that it faded from the intellectual and religious life of Europe and, though held sporadically down the centuries by a sect here and there or by a few great thinkers and mystics, it was not really restored to Western thought till it was reintroduced in the teachings of Theosophy. Now, after having been spread abroad for a century by the Theosophical Society, it is rapidly regaining its position as a world-belief.

Reincarnation has always been a characteristic part of the leading religions of the East, as every student of them knows. We cannot even think of the Brahmanical or Buddhist teachings without instantly remembering the tenet as taught therein. In Buddhism, owing among other things to its lack of bigotry, the teaching of human reimbodiment has remained closer than in any other religion to the pure form of the belief. In exoteric Brahmanism it has been greatly disfigured, as seen in one of its excrescences already noted, the erroneous doctrine of the transmigration of the human Ego into the bodies of animals.

Many of the greatest men of antiquity taught reincarnation in various forms, among them being such great names as Orpheus, Pythagoras, Empedocles, Plato, Apollonius of Tyana, with Ennius and Seneca among the Romans. We find the doctrine in ancient Persia, also among the Druids and early Nordic peoples, while it was a cornerstone of the grand mystical religion of old Egypt. In China it was a part of Taoism and its hold was deepened by the spread of Buddhism there.

In the Old Testament we find very few convincing statements even as to man's survival after death, at least not in our popular conception of immortality, thereby showing how inadequate are those scriptures, as represented by Christian tradition, to give us a truly comprehensive picture of Jewish thought at the time. For reincarnation was expounded in the Qabbâlâh, the esoteric philosophy of the Jews—their secret, mystic teaching; so did

Philo, one of the greatest philosophers belonging to the Jewish race, and a renowned Neo-Platonist, teach it. So, also, did the celebrated Jewish historian Josephus. For Josephus was a Pharisee, and he himself recorded that this body believed in and taught reincarnation.

Here and there throughout the Bible, the idea of reincarnation is seen to be in the background of the writer's or speaker's thought, as when the disciples asked Jesus: "Who did sin, this man, or his parents, that he was born blind?" (John ix:2) But how could the man have sinned, excepting in a former life, to have been *born* blind? The disciples evidently took the truth of reincarnation for granted, nor did Jesus rebuke them for this in his reply. In Matt. xi:14, Jesus said of John the Baptist: "And if ye will receive it, this is Elias, which was for to come," a statement which he seems to repeat in Mark ix:13.

These things were of course unsuspected by those earnest men of the Middle Ages (almost totally ignorant of historical developments as they were) who interpreted the Old Testament according to their own unavoidable limitations. But Theosophy calls attention to this aspect of Jewish history so long overlooked.

A true picture of the intellectual world in the early days of Christianity is illuminating indeed! Such a picture can be constructed from materials supplied by many great writers who, though knowing nothing of Theosophy (like Legge for example who wrote *Forerunners and*

Rivals of Christianity), yet present the most telling evidence that many doctrines, always considered in our education as so characteristic of Christianity, are direct or distorted reflections of the Mystery-Teachings of the Archaic Wisdom.

The two principal sources from which early Christianity derived—only to disfigure—its mystical doctrines, such as the Virgin Birth, the Passion of Christ, the Eucharist, Apostolic Succession, and others, were the Gnostic philosophy and the Mithraic Mystery Religion. These two systems were genuine developments of the primeval Esoteric Wisdom, and they flourished in the early centuries of our era. Mithraism, indeed, very nearly became the accepted religion of the Roman Empire.

The Mithraic Religion in the third century of the Christian Era had reached such a stage of development that it all but became the dominant state-religion of the then wide-flung Roman Empire. In fact, it had so much that was similar, both in doctrine and in certain forms, to early Christianity, that this fact was commented upon by all intelligent writers of the time, both Christian and 'Pagan.' As it happened, Christianity, by reason of a number of interesting causes, finally prevailed over Mithraism as the dominant religious system of Europe.

—*The Esoteric Tradition,* p. 863

With its dogmas of the vicarious atonement, salvation by faith, and the practices which grew out of these beliefs, Christianity relieved the great mass of men from strenuous moral effort and lent itself to the designs of temporal and political aggrandizement.

Reincarnation was a leading tenet of Gnosticism and formed an integral part of the Mystery Teachings of Mithraism. From these influential and popular sources it was taken over by many early Christians. Several of the greatest of the early Church Fathers, as already stated, taught it in some form—notably Bishop Synesius and, even later, Origen and Clement (later Saint Clement of the Christian Church)—all of Alexandria, and the two latter believed to have been initiated into the Mystery Schools of their day. It looks as if these wise men were striving to keep alive in the new church a link with the living Wisdom Religion. The Manicheans, a mystical sect of Hither Asia in those early days, professed reincarnation and, adopting what might be regarded as the protective coloring of Christianity, had their share in popularizing an aspect of the doctrine. This sect bore an offshoot as late as the twelfth and thirteenth centuries: the Albigenses of Languedoc, who revived the teaching. But it had then been anathema for about seven hundred years, and they were, although with difficulty, savagely exterminated.

A long list could be cited of scholars, poets, and mystics of every country and century in Europe, who have believed in and taught reincarnation. If the reader is interested, an account of them with citations in evidence of their belief will be found in two volumes, *Reincarnation, an East-West Anthology,* and *Reincarnation in World Thought,* both compiled and edited by Joseph Head and S. L. Cranston, which can be obtained from the theosophical and public libraries. The whole subject of reincarnation as a historical belief is worth looking into if only for the surprising and interesting facts, so long suppressed or forgotten, concerning the origin of what we call Christianity.

Year after year beheld the silent toil
That spread his lustrous coil;
Still, as the spiral grew,
He left the past year's dwelling for the new,
Stole with soft step its shining archway through,
Built up its idle door,
Stretched in his last-found home, and knew the
old no more. . . .

Build thee more stately mansions, O my soul!
As the swift seasons roll!
Leave thy low-vaulted past!
Let each new temple, nobler than the last,
Shut thee from heaven with a dome more vast,
Till thou at length art free,
Leaving thine outgrown shell by life's unrest-
ing sea!

—Oliver Wendell Holmes
"The Chambered Nautilus"

VIII

REINCARNATION AND DESTINY

O UR modern point of view in regard to any new 'proposition' might perhaps be summed up in the often heard query, "Where will it get me?" And characteristically, every inquirer will naturally wish to know what the individual goal is toward which this evolution of character through many lives is leading us.

One of the first changes that a study of Theosophy makes in one's outlook is that there are no absolute beginnings and no final endings to evolution or to ourselves. There are only relative beginnings and temporary endings. Everything develops by stages and it is only the forms through which these stages of evolution are accomplished that pass away. Evolution itself is periodic, as heretofore frequently noted. There is an interval of activity followed by a time of rest; and then another period of activity with its consequent period of rest. Thus onward and upward for ever.

The beginning of our period of evolution as men took place on this planet as briefly sketched in Chapter II, and more fully treated in the Manual *Man's Divine Parentage and Des-*

tiny. First came the animal soul or vesture and its physical body, builded by the lower, instinctively structural energies of Nature following the karmic lines of our planetary organism. At a certain point in this process of early development, when the animal vehicle had at last been made ready, the latent fire of mind was awakened therein by those higher Beings who had been men in a former great period of evolution.

As one candle-flame will light many others while remaining itself undiminished, so was man's mentality mystically enkindled by our more advanced, divine Brothers. Symbolically we can regard the prepared animal-physical vehicle of man as the candle, and this aggregated host of higher Beings as a great Spiritual Flame. Descending to earth, this host of divine Beings who had once been men brought *mystically* to the waiting vehicles the flame of Divine Mind. The latent faculties of the animal-man were kindled into the first feeble spark of intellect. The race then became truly human—men—thinkers, and self-conscious. They were then first able to relate themselves self-consciously to their environment. In each one awakened that particular kind of self-awareness which feels, "I am I, and no one else." From that time onward men became morally responsible for themselves, and their evolution passed from the overlordship of Nature into their own hands. Henceforth what their bodies became, in what direction their